SALTASH REMEMBERED

Douglas C. Vosper

A general view of Saltash in about 1824 which also shows a coach and cart on the horse-boat, the horses having already crossed the water.

This version of the book is virtually as originally published, presenting the work of Douglas C Vosper. There are now additional pages at the back providing information about the publisher, Arthur L Clamp.

The republishing project is being managed by Arthur's grandson, Steven Gibson. We aim to find all the research that he was involved in publishing, preserving it for the next generation as part of 'The Clamp Collection'.

INTRODUCTION

Having been asked to make available some of my photographs for A. L. Clamp to produce this pictorial record of Saltash, I hope it will prove of interest to you the viewer. I found it was not a case of what to put in, but what to leave out, but some copies will now survive many years and not get locked in some museum or other place or even get lost.

Obviously any illustrations are relatively modern for there are no illustrated records of the "Ancient Borough" story and next to nothing in writing — perhaps due to the Civil War or other fighting — of what was one of Cornwall's oldest boroughs.

Though quite a number of aerial photos of the town exist there is not one showing the whole town because part is always lost in a valley, for we have no flat land. Richard Carew in his day described the little town as being . . . *seated on the declining of a steep hill, consisting of three streets, which every shower washeth clean.* . . . Because of this the boundary of the little town was river or stream except for St. Stephens Mount, now losing its identity to Longstone. After the amalgamation with St. Stephens-by-Saltash in 1934 the position of the larger area was the same except that a second tidal river now became involved up as far as Notter Bridge.

My collection of pictures and notes has grown more in recent years. I was born at 36 St. Stephens Road, then the last building on that side of the road before reaching St. Stephens School. During two World Wars the first created a trench-protected army base camp and in the second the enemy left their marks, especially in Fore Street; but cameras were not allowed! Save for one pre-1859 photo, the coming of the railway seems to have introduced the use of the camera with its slow exposures and then, at the turn of the century, came the picture postcard.

Early on the town had various names but the last one used before the word Saltash was *Essa*, taken from the family called Esse, Essa or Ashe who in the twelfth century had the manor at or near Ashtor Rock, where our pillar of the Royal Albert Bridge stands. Queen Elizabeth I in her 1584 charter refers to the fact that *Essa is now commonly called Saltash*, yet John Leyland used Asche in the mid-1500s.

It was this Ashtor area protruding into the River Tamar — Cornwall's Celtic boundary — that brought protection and the width of the estuary down to a thousand odd feet (300 metres). For this reason Saltash became the mud-less crossing place from earliest times. As wheeled vehicles became more usable what was called a horse-boat came into use and then, in December 1832, the first wooden steam ferry was introduced, dragging itself along chains. This then was the traffic crossing until October, 1961, when the Tamar Bridge came into use.

In 1801 buildings higher than the Commercial Hotel (now Brunel) were almost non-existent, but with the coming of the railway some new buildings were constructed. This increased enough for a local train service from the Plymouth area to start in 1904 with a motor bus continuing to Callington and Albaston. The great increase in car ownership and the coming of the road bridge really let housing run wild and many many acres of good and bad farmland — even bog and steep valley sides — have gone to builders. Go toward Longlands and look back! North of New Road does still have a restriction order, at any rate until a new road is built.

Old Saltash revolved around the river; lack of foresight allowed Waterside's individual people, its houses and courtyards to be swept away. Polperro and St Ives were similar and are now tourist attractions, not just another town for the visitor to pass through.

I hope these pictures will bring back memories and to others interest in Saltash as it was during the last eighty years and more.

Douglas C. Vosper.

Mr. Harris delivering coal. The passage between Rose Hill entrance wall and shop gave right of way to Avondale Cottage behind and to five two-room cottages backing onto those seen here, facing Fore Street until the blitz. They were built to house Brunel's men.

A 1906 photo showing this building standing in Archway Field. Replaced by present building (old Y.M.C.A.) opened by Lady Beatrice Pole Carew on 13th October, 1910, this now awaits its fate for road widening among other things. Belle View is to the left.

Oldest known Saltash photo. To the left entrance is the present car park of Commercial Hotel (Brunel 1961). Suitable for pack horses the white part of archway house was removed in 1859, it was a hindrance to loaded vehicles from the new station.

On the left is the old Y.M.C.A., then Stephens (butcher), one of the town's old slate hung buildings replaced in 1932. Right is Squire's coach builders showroom (no. 90) converted to the fire station, 15th November, 1927. Then can be seen Blewett (shoemaker) the new Midland Bank and the Commercial Hotel.

Coronation procession in 1937 showing Sergeant Leach, Mace bearers Saunders and Southern, Mayor E. Webber, Deputy H. J. Davy and Councillors going to the old Methodist Chapel now the Post Office. Buildings are the London Central Meat Co., National Provincial Bank, Goodman's Dairy, Post Office and Dingle's stationers.

Taken about 1910 showing on right Dingle's stationery shop. Beyond is the entrance to "The Mansion" now the Working Men's Club. Opposite, being taken in, is Paine's wine delivery hand cart, then Luxton's shoe shop and the Post Office.

THE LAST VISIBLE RELIC OF TUDOR SALTASH STILL STANDING IN FORE STREET.
(Photo by Mr. D. Freeman.)

The site of 105 Fore Street now part of the Co-op property, this building had no locks on its doors only very large bolts. Remembered as Widdecombe's Bakery it was taken by E. Goad (upholsterer) who lost his family when it and the buildings opposite were destroyed during the blitz of 28th April, 1941.

In 1890 the Devon and Cornwall Bank put up a building, 97-98 Fore Street. No. 98 was the Post Office. A Mr. F. A. Rawling was in charge of both. In 1923 the Post Office vacated the building which was then Lloyd's Bank. The photograph below shows greenstone and granite boundary stones of the *Cornish Patch* in Devon from 1329 to 1895. They are near the Cornwall Gate inn.

The flat part of Fore Street, showing some pre-war shops such as Nicholson's, which one entered up steps, and others down. Road was 16-19 ft. overall and in summer the dust was laid by a four-wheeled water cart filled at Adit Lane.

Herbert Simons' grocery shop on the corner of North Road about 1910, next to Clarke's three shops. Railway Hotel on the left is next to P. E. B. Porter's office and Jane the butcher. The narrow street numbers are up the north side and down the other.

The 1959 shambles at Simon's Corner, only Rounsefell's shop withstood the blitz. Clarkes were granted a temporary cafe to help feeding after the war. The area was removed in 1961 and the railed off piece was later laid out with seats and a bust of Brunel.

The entrance of North Road about 1912. Buildings left from roundabout are much as today, but then it was Visick, jeweller, and Pope, costumier. Right is now pushed back into a green rest area. Perillie ice cream cart is flanked by Stanlakes dairy and Porter, solicitor.

Woman with two earthenware pitchers going to fetch water from the spring or well situated under the wall at end of railings. Old Buscundle Cottages in on the right were replaced in 1971.

All the buildings on the right to where lamp post cuts the sky were removed including Masonic Hall (old Chapel) and Rosecliffe in 1959 for building the road bridge. The cobble stone pavement was removed in 1921 as work for the unemployed.

Our Guildhall was built in 1890 from the open side of Market House and Assembly Room. During 1923-24 this was replanned bringing the door to the west and rebuilding the first floor. Re-opened on 6th February, 1925, it was largely rebuilt again with ferry compensation money in 1967. The Mayor L. G. Davey, Deputy J. Foster, Town clerk A. G. Bellingham, Town sergeant W. A. Lee and Mace bearer P. Petryna can be seen in the lower photograph assembling for the last Borough council meeting held on 12th March, 1974.

Among the Charters granted to Saltash over the centuries is that of the Reincorporation dated 7th June, 1774, from King George III. Straw coloured in bees wax is the Great Seal of Great Britain, one side shows the king on his horse, the other his crowning(?).

As the first Mayor mentioned in the Charter of 1774, Bradshaw presented this red, green and gold minute book to the Borough. The 20 inch long silver maces are dated 1623. The 7½ inch one of 1760 was used by the Town Sergeant as an emblem of authority when making arrests within *The Liberty of the Water Tamar*.

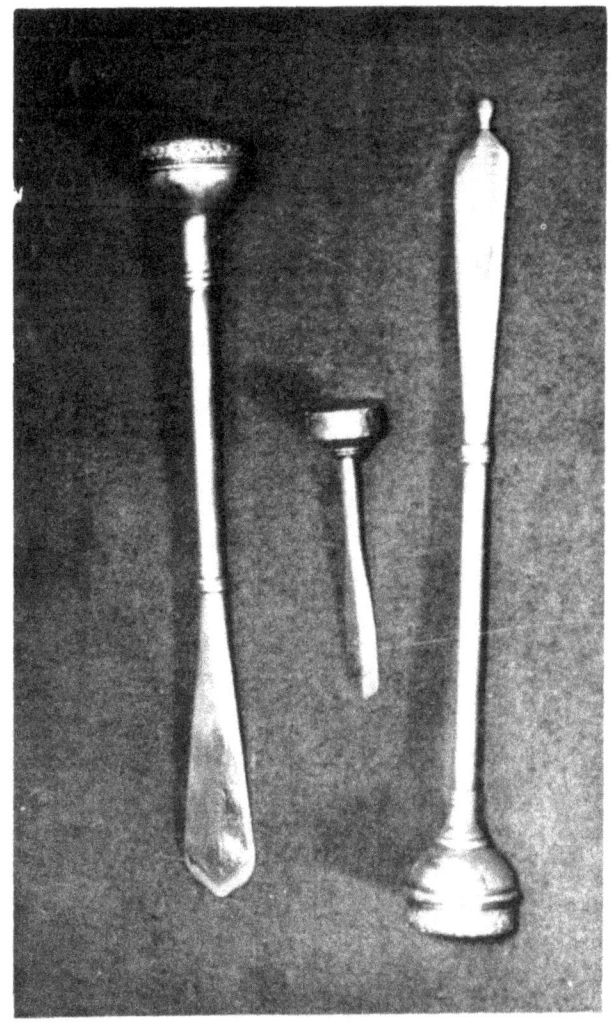

Centre pier of bridge ready 1856 and a 455 ft., 500/600 ton truss, ready for floating out on 1st September, 1857. The first truss was in place July, 1858, and this unusual suspension bridge with its two spans was opened on 2nd May, 1859. The first through train ran on 12th April, 1859.

A three-master of some size can be seen on town beach in the 1900s. The white building with six windows had three entrances at different levels from Silver Street. Ashtor Wharf below the bridge and Waterside are still intact. In the foreground is the London and South Western Railway (1890) boundary fence.

Great celebrations took place at Saltash for the Centenary of the opening of Brunel's world famous bridge and the opening of the Cornwall Railway. The "Special" in the station, 1st May, 1959, is the locomotive G.W.R. 5069 *Isambard Kingdom Brunel*.

Gelignite was fired in 1906 to bring down the stone road bridge for lengthening the "up" platform. The steel bridge can be seen already in place and cut stone being saved, 50 tons of wood were used to receive the 150 tons of stone.

The Cornwall Railway's trestle viaduct across the mouth of Forder Creek at Antony Passage in about 1900. Until 1908 the line, with a number of these bridges, followed the river from Saltash as far as St. Germans.

A pre-1906 photo of the building of the stone viaduct over Forder Creek when the Great Western Railway brought a double track line further inland. The first goods train ran over it on 23rd March, 1908. Note the railway trucks in use above the water.

St. Nicholas and Faith Church, the tower over north transept is rare in Cornwall. Battlements were removed in 1930, clock dates from 1730. Last trees of Chapel Yard were removed in 1962. The Church Rooms to the right replaced the old National School and to the left is the Vicarage wall.

North Road about 1910 used to be *Old Mill Lane*. These shops then Essa Cycle and Car Works and A. Irwin, baker, together with gardens and a house or two, were removed early in 1960 to make way for the road bridge.

This was erected as the Board School in North Road to replace the National School adjoining St. Nicholas Church until 1870. Twice enlarged it became a Public Elementary (known as Council Schools) in 1919 and, in 1957, the Secondary Modern School. It was largely burnt down in 1975.

An aerial view of Waterside, the bridge and the ferry. Also to be seen is a pump house on both pier and quay used for pumping water about the town for war-time fire fighting. Across the river is an oil fuelling jetty and landing craft ramps or "hards" used to load American soldiers from the huts (top right) for D-Day, 1944. Below can be seen the Mayor, M. Huggins, civic officers and local dignitories arriving for the last (Civic) ferry trip on 24th October, 1961.

Right: **Tamar Street** decorated with foliage for Queen Victoria's Diamond Jubilee in 1897. Below is shown Mary Newman's Cottage in about 1900, first wife of Francis Drake. A tablet was placed here on 25th August, 1930. The building is preserved and was made over to Caradon District Council in February, 1975. Drake like Hawkins and others must have walked the little streets, for they brought their ships up the Tamar to shelter from enemies and the weather. Also, in about 1910, Mary Ann Pope can be seen at her cockle window in Tamar Street — almost a self-contained shopping street. The doorway, dated 1584, was set up incorrectly in the rebuilding of 1963-4.

North end of Tamar Street was pulled down 1961 with the arch-way house featured in Turner's painting now in the U.S.A. Extended sills were used, on which to stand large plates and bowls of cockles, winkles, mussels, oysters, crabs and shrimps from the river. Outsiders used to know it as *Picklecock Alley*. Above the girl on the left is a barber's coloured pole. Below shows King Cockle at Winkle Fair, an idea thought up for Waterside during 1951-4. Mayor Miss W. M. Fernside — our first lady Mayor — can also be seen with Douglas Marshall, M.P. and Jester Ivy Train.

Knife grinder. These were very common in towns sharpening a wide variety of knives, scissors and cutting tools. Years ago when only sandstone and not emery wheels were used, the apparatus had to include a tray of water for cooling.

A lamb on one of two boggy greens (Maybrook Drive area) of the 18 hole Saltash Golf Course, running from 1924 until the war. Later it had become 9 holes due to the building of Warfelton Crescent. Warfelton Farm is seen to right on Church Road.

A boat without its flag, from one of the many boating clubs in the town during the 1920s and even 1930s. They were run by churches, Y.M.C.A., Essa R.C., etc. The stern board was often carved with raised letters. This shows a six-oar galley or gig.

Commercial Wharf at a regatta about 1905. At the top right, not the *Mount Edgcumbe*, but H.M.S. *Implacable* brought up river to have its bottom scraped on the mud flats. It could be the bows of *Goss Hawk*, the *Mount Edgcumbe's* training ship seen at the top centre.

A "Tea Treat" thought to have been at Wearde House, — everyone can be seen in their *besties*. Usually run by Church Sunday Schools they gave many children their only chance of a visit to the country years ago.

Saltash Steamboat Co's *Princess Royal* well packed with a popular Sunday School outing — she was licenced to take 462 persons. Ahead and still on the Devon side is the Industrial Training Ship *Mount Edgcumbe*. Taken on 22nd July, 1908, this postcard is postmarked 24th July, 1908!

Taken in 1920 with tide out and limekiln beyond barge. Behind the railings the left hand house was a shop; the cottages on right were pulled down in 1966-7, behind which stood a mill. Chapel closed in 1974 after 128 years being there when 'roadway' moved from beach to its present site.

Rickards of Callington ran horse buses regularly to Saltash station, this two-horse vehicle has Jim Rickard "up". Of special interest to-day is the state of the road, the primitive brake mechanism and a seat at the back above the step.

On the road about 1910 the Albert Hall (lower Fore Street) Mission Band on their summer outing in I.Q. Betty's waggonette! Note the man with cornet above nearest candle lamp of which there are three, one for seeing the horses.

Spooner's of Plymouth caravan with naphtha lamps hanging from tailboard visiting the district. Seen here in "The Park", now Victoria Road area, and behind is the Wesleyan Chapel — now the Post Office. Buildings in Fore Street seen down today's Wesley Road.

Factory made prefabricated bungalows to house people temporarily were erected after the Second World War. These at Longview Road were replaced by Police houses in 1970; others were at Moorland Lane and the now Warfelton Gardens. Dates were from 1945-67.

Burraton Cross in the early 1900s showing F. Hearl's saddler and ironmonger shop. There was no change until Snell's butcher shop on the left came down for road improvements about 1937. The gardens ahead and the wall opposite have since gone.

Snell's new butchers shop on the right looks upon Mrs. Cook's cows ambling across Burraton Cross from grazing at Homer Park to The Elms for milking soon after 1952. More traffic changes were made and then the traffic lights were working by 29th January, 1962.

Vaughan's Brewery as depicted on a card across from the Drill Hall. Pale ale was 54/- per Barrel! Their bottles can still be dug up around the town. Among its various uses was a slaughter house, stable, electric works, laundry and an ironmongery, almost all of which, including the chimney, was cleared to make way for the road bridge. To the left can be seen the start of an adit made in Dartmouth slate below Lower Port View, north of the old boundary stone by Coombe stream. To the right is a well or flooded ice chamber of Alexandra House against Albert Road, once known as Middle Street. The piece of wood shows the top of a 5 ft. deep water hole, 4 ft. in width in a T-shaped chamber. It is now lost under a car park, 1963.

In 1959 the Tamar Road Bridge was started. The top illustration shows the roundabout taking shape on the 18th June, 1961, and the shaded area shows where North Road ran from Fore Street. Below left the first of the steel trusses is about to be lifted from the river, 11th March, 1961, a method of construction pioneered for the larger Severn and Forth Bridges soon to be built. Traffic can be seen using one side on 24th October, 1961. Fifty houses and ten shops were demolished to make way for this development.

The first tent camp at Cross Park Wearde Road of the King's Own (Royal Lancaster Regiment). Beyond the trees a camp of huts was then erected and the East Surrey Regiment took over for the rest of the war. After that it became a convalescent camp with the men in light blue. Removed in 1927-8, one hut still survives as St. Stephens Hall.

Wearde House, built about 1740, and when empty in 1903 workmen cooked food there and later the roof was seen to be alight. Fire brigade found no water pressure so what was saved was largely due to a bucket chain from the river, formed by sailors from H.M.S. *Defiance*.

H.M.S. *Defiance* (1861) Torpedo School first moved to Wearde Quay in 1884 where there was a Custom Post and gate. The other ships in the group in 1929 were *Andromeda* (1897), *Vulcan* (1889), *Inconstant* (1868). The school moved to Will Cove in 1930.

St. Barnabas Cottage Hospital, a valued part of Saltash, built for Mrs. Caroline Ley during 1887 as a memorial to her husband. Run by Sisters of St. Margarets, East Grinstead, until taken over by the National Health Service on 31st December, 1955. No maternity unit there now.

G.W.R. motor bus No. 11 of their Saltash Station/Callington and Albaston service started on 1st June, 1904. The two galvanised sheds still stand at the old goods yard. Behind are houses of Lower Port View, that on the right being "The Towers". Driver is Mr. Hewitt.

No. 26 a G.W.R. 24hp Miln-Daimler coming up from the goods yard with Pat Cummins and Harry Dance about 1905. Note the radiator in front of engine cover. Right of way seen along the outside of Coombe viaduct closed in 1965. Bull Point jetty is in the back ground.

An early nineteenth century print looking from Forder, drawn for Jedediah S. Tucker who was still at the Castle in 1856. The fortification, belonging to the Duchy of Cornwall, was last in action during the Prayer Book Rebellion of 1549. The map to the left clearly shows the Borough's size in about 1801 and the lack of buildings away from the three streets. The Borough held rights over *The Liberty of the Waters Tamar* from outside the Breakwater to points inland except Sutton Pool and Lary. Shown below are the letters "SB" at Okeltor above Calstock.

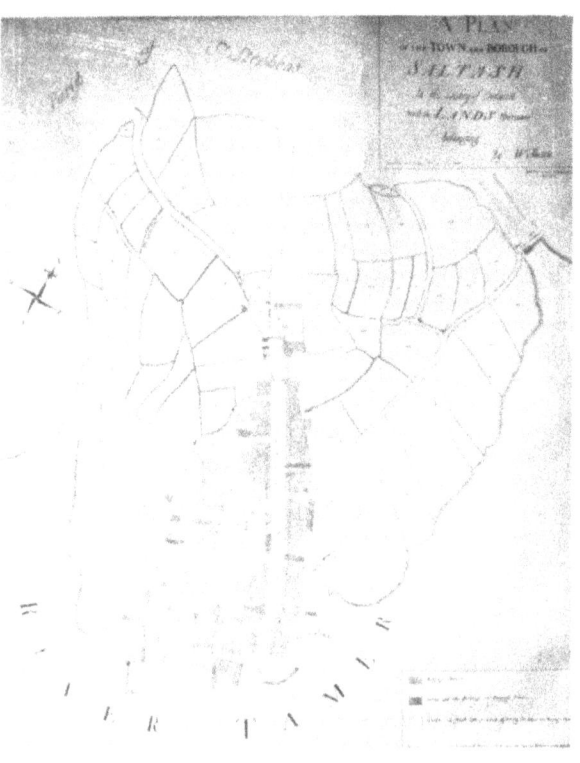

Arthur L. Clamp – the man behind the books

Arthur Leslie Clamp was a man of boundless energy with a passion for helping others, particularly through his love of history. A printer by trade, he started his career in a printing company before moving his family from Exeter to Plymouth to teach at the Plymouth College of Art and Design, where he eventually became the Head of the Printing Department.

A Devoted Family Man

Arthur with his five children.

Despite his love of teaching, Arthur prioritised his family, always making it home by 5:30pm for tea. He and his wife, Rosemary, raised five children: Susan, Angela, Elizabeth, David, and Steven. Arthur would often combine his love of family and history by taking his children on Sunday walks, encouraging them to appreciate historical monuments by taking photos or making crayon rubbings of gravestones for his books. The family home at 203 Elburton Road was a hub of activity, with a large garden, featuring a two-storey fort and a makeshift swimming pool.

A Lifelong Learner and Adventurer

Arthur's thirst for knowledge extended beyond history to a deep curiosity about the world. He was passionate about exploring different cultures, traditions, and cuisines, often taking advantage of his long summer holidays as a teacher to travel to places like India, Russia, South America, the middle east and the USA, sometimes bringing one of his children along. This adventurous spirit even influenced his home life, as seen by the short-lived family tradition of steam-cooking vegetables after a trip to Iceland.

History is a prominent feature of family days out

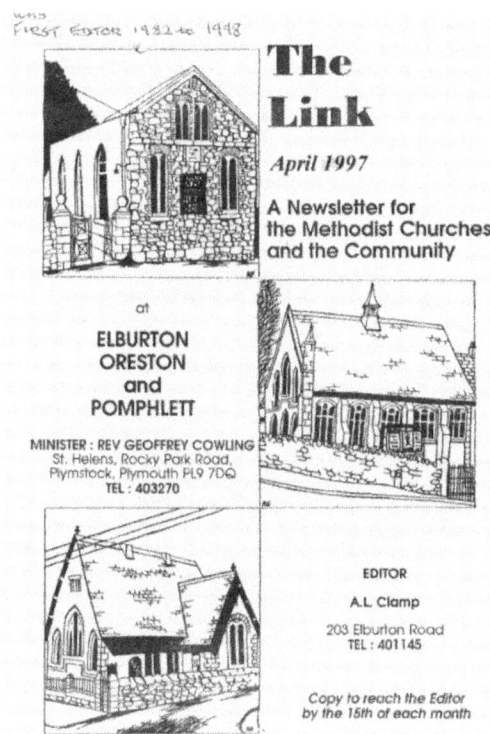

First Editor 1982 to 1998

Community and Philanthropic Spirit

His commitment to serving others was evident in his long-standing involvement with the Elburton Methodist Church. He was the Sunday School Superintendent for over 15 years and served as the editor of the wider church's monthly newsletter, "The Link," for a similar duration. After Rosemary's very sad passing, Arthur later remarried and, following a chance encounter with a professor from India, established a connection with a missionary school in Chennai. Together with his new wife, Christine, he co-founded a "Sponsor a Child's Education" program that continues to this day.

*Pictured left – The cover of 'The Link' complete
with hand drawn sketches of each church by Angela
Below right – Arthur Clamp promoting his latest book
Below left – Arthur at home with his first wife, Rosemary
Below centre – Arthur on holiday with his second wife,
Christine*

A Legacy of Learning and Positivity

Arthur's greatest passion was history, which he brought to life through tireless research, documentation, and the many books he authored. He was driven by a need to "never be stuck in a rut," constantly seeking new experiences, meeting new people, and expanding his knowledge. With a positive attitude and a great sense of humour, he was always ready to help others, leaving a lasting impact on his family and community. His children, Susan, Angela, Elizabeth, David, and Steven, remember him with love and gratitude.

David Clamp, 2025

A Legacy of Local History

Below is the story of how Arthur L Clamp began writing books, in his own words, drafted shortly before he passed away in 2001. I have only made minor alterations to this text, correcting grammatical errors that he did not survive to correct himself. When I first discovered this text, I was shocked to see my name mentioned. It seems that, unbeknownst to me, I shared my first PC with him. I suspect he used it during the day when I was at school, although I do have one memory of sitting with him and showing him how it worked. It has been a pleasure to pick up where he left off and see his books republished and redistributed, and to know that I was part of the story, even back then. It was also fascinating to discover that his pricing structure matches the way I have tried to price the books, with a third going to local sellers and the rest covering printing costs with a little left over for my expenses.

I am his eldest grandson, and it is a privilege to curate his legacy, which we are calling 'The Clamp Collection'. The very last line of the text originally reads "The following pages list all the titles." Sadly, that page is missing and we have no record of all the books he published and knowing that some of those were researched by other authors makes the process of finding them even harder. I look forward to one day completing the collection and seeing them all available again. And maybe, one day, I'll even start writing my own to add to the series. For now, here is his story in his own words.

Steven Gibson, 2025

Writing and Publishing Booklets on Local Topics and Areas

I started this interest in either 1968 or 1969 when living in Woodford. I had by these dates established the Department of Printing and I think I must have been looking for something different to do. The first titles were of A5 size proofed from type set at Clarke, Doble and Brendon, Ltd., Plymouth printers, and then made up into pages and printed at Sawtell and Neilson, Ltd., Totnes.

Then began a slow process of getting them out to shops, etc. which proved to be more time consuming and difficult than actually researching, writing and getting the books into print. However, I persisted and opened a business account with Barclays Bank on the Broadway. I was advised to give it a title so I called it "Westway Publications". There came along another problem, one of storage of paper and finished books which was solved when the family moved to Elburton in 1970.

I changed the printer to Penwell, Ltd., Callington, Cornwall, as he was then just setting up himself and his prices seemed very reasonable. I did not get any of the printers to make up the complete books. I hand folded the flat printed sheets, stitched the books on a small manual table stitcher and trimmed them in a small hand turned guillotine which I bought from someone in Penzance for £40. It was brought up in a van.

The trouble and time going to and fro to Callington was too much so I transferred the printing to PDS Printers, Prince Rock, Plymouth, and I have been with them ever since. Now they are at Plympton which is easy to reach and they fold the flat sheets which was turning out to be a long chore which only saved a small part of the printing costs.

All my first titles were written by myself. I took the photographs and developed them in the loft of the house, the type was set by now on a computer situated in the house at Elburton from which I had collected photographic lengths of text to cut up and law down as pages.

At some point I decided that I would do my own film processing of lith film so I bought a large second hand process camera from Kingsbridge and learnt through trial and error to make line negatives of the text and halftone negatives of the illustrations which proved more difficult than I anticipated. The main problem was trying to keep the developer in the large dish at the correct temperature as any change would affect the developing time. I replaced this old camera with a brand new one bought from Croydon, Surrey, costing £900. This has turned out to be a great asset cutting out an expensive part of the printer's costs and one crucial aspect of the work which I could control.

By the middle 1970s there were many outlets I had contacted in Plymouth, up to Dartmoor, Exeter, around to Torbay, Totnes, Dartmouth and the South Hams. The market for local books was much greater than I had first thought and through getting to know many local people undertaking research themselves had the chance to help and make up books for other people who had in most instances, got together a collection of photographs with some text in a rather muddled way. Through my experience in print I was able to shape up their work and get it into print and in every case I had to pay the printer and let the person have the royalties. In the majority of titles produced in this manner this was another way of producing titles and it did give some profit to my work. However, I must say that in a few cases I lost out by either the other person getting the numbers wrong, not returning any monies from stock I delivered or they thought that more of their books should have been sold.

The print run was usually 1,000 copies and from time to time I have had reprints of 250 copies. It took about ten years to clear the first print run so I always had large stocks in the garage, workshop, etc. The numbers sold during the early years was about 7,000 copies a year increasing to around 9,000 copies and for the whole of the enterprise about 500,000 have been sold. The booklets have become part of the local scene and many people collect them, shops regularly order copies and I go around certain areas month by month restocking or replacing titles as necessary.

During the past year or so I have started setting the text on a Packard Bell PC, something which I should have done some years back. I share it with Steven Gibson, my grandson. There appears to be no end to the market for local books, but I could not earn a regular income because of the long time it takes to sell stock.

However, now exceeding 100 titles made up mainly of A4 twenty-four page booklets, some folded guides, with selling prices set with a third going to the shop which is the trade custom, the original idea has been quite successful and could go on for ever.

Apart from monetary benefits, however spasmodically these might be, I have learnt a lot myself, met many interesting people and have become part of the local scene with requests to give talks and to advise people about getting into print.

Arthur L Clamp, 2001

This newspaper article, published by the Evening Herald on 17th August 2001, forms a good record of his life. Just as he encourages us to learn more about local history, we encourage you to learn a little about him. For that reason, we have included these pages at the back of all the most recently republished books, in honour of his memory and recognition of his contribution to the community.

www.ingramcontent.com/pod-product-compliance
Lightning Source LLC
Chambersburg PA
CBHW061408070526

44584CB00031B/4188